The Self-Help Guide to Stress Management

Anthony Parnell, M.S.W.

Author of *Healing through Writing and I AM...Success*

Books by Anthony Parnell

Las Vegas, Nevada

The Self-Help Guide to Stress Management

Copyright © 2021 by Anthony Parnell

All rights reserved. No part of this book may be reproduced in any form or by any means without permission in writing from the publisher.

ISBN# 978-0-9644205-8-8

Library of Congress Control Number: 2021900043

Printed in the United States of America

Cover Design by Joshua Lewis and Pabrita Halder

Edited by Stephen Silke and Paul Morehouse, PhD

Additional Contributions by Yurnell Jackson

DISCLAIMER:

It is strongly recommended that physicians and other health professionals be consulted in addition to incorporating the philosophy and techniques offered here in *The Self-Help Guide to Stress Management*. Further, if you are experiencing extreme difficulty performing normal tasks or coping with situations at home or work, it is strongly recommended that a mental health professional be consulted. The "Additional Resources" section of this book provides professional referral information as well as sources for more detailed information on stress and other health related questions.

*Learning to live a life
of love,
balance,
harmony,
and shared abundance
is the essence of life.*

Everything else is secondary.

Anthony Parnell

CONTENTS

The Importance of Self-Help in Stress Management..................................1

The Concept of Balance and Well-Being 5

A Basic Understanding of Stress 13

PART I: 10 STRATEGIES FOR EFFECTIVELY MANAGING STRESS..19

Strategy Number 1: Accept that Stress Management is a Lifestyle that Requires You to be Proactive rather than Reactive 21

Strategy Number 2: Be Consistent in Setting Aside an Adequate Amount of Time to be Alone and in Silence (for Self-Reflection) 25

Strategy Number 3: Be Honest with Yourself on a Daily Basis and in All Situations 31

Strategy Number 4: Accept that Balance Can Be Achieved Only When There is an Equal Commitment to Your Mind, Body and Spirit 35

Strategy Number 5: Exercise Discipline in Working towards Large Goals By First Disciplining Yourself in Accomplishing Small Goals.....39

Strategy Number 6: Maintain Balance in Your Personal and professional lives by Identifying and Utilizing Tangible and Intangible Resources (Physical, Social, Psychological, Material) 45

Strategy Number 7: Minimize Physical Clutter in Your Home and Workplace 49

Strategy Number 8: Be Consistent in Surrounding Yourself and Interacting with Positive People 53

Strategy Number 9: Financially Prepare for Economic Downturns, Job Layoffs, and/or Retirement 57

Strategy Number 10: Develop an Emergency Preparedness Plan in the Event of a Natural Disaster and/or Other Unexpected Environmental, National or Global Crisis...63

Self-Graded Chart 70

PART II: APPLYING THE "10 STRATEGIES" TO EVERYDAY LIFE 73

Step Number 1: Maintain a Commitment to "5 Minutes a Day" of Writing and Self-Reflection 77

Step Number 2: Identify Warning Signs & Stressors 83

Step Number 3: Develop Prioritized Stress Management Goals 95

Step Number 4: Identify Internal & External Resources 111

Step Number 5: Putting It All Together (Maintaining an Effective Stress Management Plan) 119

Appendix A: Self-Exploratory Questions 123

Appendix B: "Stress Management Report Card" 125

Appendix C: "5 Minutes a Day" of Writing & Self-Reflection 127

Appendix D: Maintenance Plan for Decluttering Physical Environment 129

Appendix E: Self-Care Monitoring Chart 139

Appendix F: Affirmations for Minimizing Stress 141

Appendix G: Exercise for Surrounding Yourself with Positive People 143

Appendix H: 7 Key Elements to Organizational Change 147

Appendix I: Eight Variables Related to Job Satisfaction and Functioning Effectively in the Workplace 149

Additional Resources 153

References and Further Reading 157

The Importance of Self-Help in Stress Management

Millions of Americans are in need of tools and strategies that will enable them to manage the stress they experience in their everyday life.

According to APA's 2019 *Stress in America* survey:

- More than three-quarters of adults report physical or emotional symptoms of stress, such as headache, feeling tired or changes in sleeping habits.

- Nearly 3 in 5 adults say they could have used more emotional support in the last year.

- Nearly half of adults say they have laid awake at night because of stress in the prior month.

- 6 in 10 adults identify work (64%) and money (60%) as significant sources of stress, making work and money the most commonly mentioned personal stressors.

    (https://www.apa.org/news/press/releases/stress/2019/stress-america-2019.pdf)

The Self-Help Guide to Stress Management

As a mental health professional for more than 20 years, I am fully aware that many individuals who are in need of stress management do not seek help due to a sense of shame or embarrassment. My experience has also been that individuals who seek professional help due to feeling overwhelmed by stress, frequently fail to recognize the extent to which they can help themselves.

My goal in writing this book is to help you tap into your own sense of Self and learn to identify and utilize the internal resources that you already possess; inherent skills available to you that will come to the surface as you begin to make the effort to effectively manage your stress. Thus, this book places an emphasis on the concept of self-help which, essentially, places a priority on you doing everything within your power to maintain a sense of work-life balance.

In using the term "self-help," I am not suggesting that you should refrain from consulting with a medical or mental health professional if you are feeling overwhelmed with stress. Rather, what I am suggesting is that the internal resources you identify and develop on your own can and should be used to reinforce and supplement the interventions of a mental health or medical professional.

A perfect example of this would be to begin exercising discipline toward setting aside a regular time to be alone, in silence, for self-reflection. Why is this so important? Because, apart from any interventions a therapist or doctor can provide, self-awareness is necessary to be in tune with the ever-changing needs of your mind, body and spirit and to help prepare yourself to respond accordingly.

Anthony Parnell, M.S.W.

This book will guide you through the process of developing greater self-awareness. Additionally, it will provide you with specific tools and strategies that you can begin implementing immediately in your efforts to effectively manage stress in your personal and professional lives.

The Concept of Balance and Well-Being

Before jumping into an in-depth discussion of stress and how to minimize it in your personal and professional lives, I think it's important to first spend some time talking about the concept of "Balance and Well-Being."

The word "balance" as used throughout this book is never meant to indicate a fixed state of existence. Rather, it is meant to indicate the active and ongoing process of maintaining awareness of Self and responding appropriately to one's self-care needs. Just as the human body has a temperature range that must be maintained for optimal performance, so do our personal and professional lives. We each have a different capacity for juggling multiple routine tasks and responsibilities without feeling overloaded or compromised. However, if our self-awareness is limited or we are not fully honest with ourselves when our stress levels begin to exceed our normal capacity, we run the risk of falling out of balance.

Self-awareness and honesty with oneself are paramount to minimizing stress and therefore maintaining balance in one's life. As a result, the two most significant concepts or tools that I will stress throughout this book are: writing/journaling and self-reflection. For nearly 30 years, I have experienced significant benefits by utilizing these tools in my personal life. This is combined with more than two decades of professional experience as a mental health therapist, social worker and workshop facilitator helping others identify and utilize healthy methods for coping with stress and maintaining balance in their personal and professional lives.

The emotional and spiritual benefits of writing and self-reflection on a daily or consistent basis are described in detail in my book, Healing through Writing: *A Journaling Guide to Emotional and Spiritual Growth* (2020). In *Healing through Writing,* I present examples of various methods of journal writing, techniques for developing greater self-awareness, and a self-inventory tool for monitoring emotional and spiritual growth through what I call, "Seven Determinants of Emotional and Spiritual Growth." *The Self-Help Guide to Stress Management* is an extension of the philosophy and techniques of *Healing through Writing* in that it provides a step-by-step approach to expanding self-awareness and maintaining balance and well-being. It also offers a framework for viewing balance as a multi-dimensional element of our human make-up (mind, body and spirit) and personal growth as a continuous cycle fueled by an individual's level of commitment.

My personal and professional experiences have affirmed that the ability to maintain balance and well-being in an individual's personal and professional lives is a skill acquired over time. One, therefore, does not simply read a book to learn how to maintain balance and well-being. Rather, you must make conscious commitments to stay focused on discipline, self-reflection, ritual and holistic beliefs. Two of the most essential building blocks for maintaining balance and well-being are: first, develop the discipline to incorporate a routine of self-reflection and other rituals into your daily life and, secondly, adopt holistic beliefs that encompass an awareness of mind, body and spirit.

The Self-Help Guide to Stress Management was specifically designed as a combination of textbook and workbook so that, beyond receiving valuable information and guidance, you are challenged to commit to writing and self-exploration on a daily basis as a means to effectively managing stress and facilitating personal growth. Once those building blocks are in place, it is much easier to develop and maintain a proactive lifestyle that promotes balance and well-being.

PART 1 of *The Self-Help Guide to Stress Management* begins with an outline and description of ten strategies for effectively managing stress. You are encouraged to examine strengths and weaknesses in your lifestyle – habits of daily living – as it relates to each of these strategies. More specifically, these 10 Strategies will become the guideposts that encourage you to write reflections (make journal entries) on your thoughts, emotions and life experiences. Writing regularly provides a means of gaining greater clarity in your beliefs and in your ability to identify internal and external obstacles thereby helping you to achieve balance and well-being in daily life. For you to maximize the benefits of this book, you must concurrently record your thoughts, emotions and reflections in a journal of your choice be it hardbound, a spiral notebook, a 3-ring binder, or other durable books that inspires and retains your creative writing.

PART 2 provides an opportunity for you to practice utilizing and incorporating the "10 Strategies" into your daily life. This includes writing clear stress management goals, prioritizing those goals and identifying internal and external resources that will aid you in accomplishing them.

7 Core Concepts that support the successful achievement of Stress Management

On the following page are brief descriptions, of seven core concepts that are not only critical in helping us understand *stress* but also two important antidotes to stress, *balance and well-being*. After you read each description, I invite you to pause for a few moments and reflect on the broader meaning of the word so as to nurture a deeper sense of it. Also, to further reinforce your understanding of each concept, space has been provided on the following pages so that you can write down any life experience, thought or emotion that may be triggered by, or related to, any of these concepts. Note: By taking advantage of this initial opportunity to write in the book, you take an important first step that can help you begin to make regular journal entries.

STRESS – The nonspecific response of the body to any demand, whether it is caused by, or results in, pleasant or unpleasant conditions (Selye, 1956, p. 74).

BALANCE – A condition of stability brought about by the inner and outer work that an individual puts forth to achieve and sustain a consistent flow of positive energy in one's daily life. BALANCE can be achieved by strengthening one's ability to cope with the predictable and unpredictable demands that naturally occur in one's personal and professional lives.

SELF-AWARENESS – A high level of self-perception brought about through an individual's ability to assess the degree of stress in their life or, in other words, measure their own sense of BALANCE (see above). An individual's SELF-AWARENESS often reflects the number of internal and external resources they can identify and utilize to help minimize the normal wear and tear of stress to their mind, body and spirit. SELF-AWARENESS also reflects an ability to independently explore and understand the source of one's thoughts, emotions and behavior.

EMPOWERMENT – The ability of an individual to utilize the internal and external resources that have been identified to improve one's life situation and to maintain balance and well-being in one's personal and professional lives (Anthony Parnell, *Healing Through Writing*, 2020).

SPIRITUALITY – One's awareness of the Universal Life Force that creates and sustains all things; one's ability to utilize this awareness to grow in love, expand consciousness, and to fulfill one's life purpose (Anthony Parnell, *Healing Through Writing*, 2020).

HEALING – The process of restoring health and balance to one's mind, body and spirit; addressing unmet physical, emotional and spiritual needs (Anthony Parnell, *Healing Through Writing*, 2020).

WHOLENESS – A condition of BALANCE, SELF-AWARENESS AND EMPOWERMENT. WHOLENESS is achieved through an individual's ability to effectively process (bring clarity to) one's thoughts and emotions and to respond effectively to life situations and to others without being fragmented or limited by gender, race, age or other falsely perceived conditions of limitation.

The Self-Help Guide to Stress Management

Personal Reflection

Anthony Parnell, M.S.W.

Personal Reflection

A Basic Understanding of Stress

The complexity of the phenomenon of stress can be evidenced by the myriad of life challenges with which we must contend on a daily basis – financial challenges, personal and job-related problems and so on. Even more, the culture of our modern society has evolved such that we are bombarded and frequently overwhelmed by demands on our time and energy. Indeed, stress is a common factor in everyone's life, rising up often quickly and unexpectedly. Interestingly, we all experience and respond to stressful life situations in our own unique way. While the birth of a child induces an overwhelming financial and emotional strain on some, others may experience a sense of spiritual joy and fulfillment *despite the financial and emotional sacrifice!* This is the irony of stress: it has negative as well as positive qualities and its impact varies from person to person.

The broad scope of stress makes the concept of "balance" and "self-awareness" extremely important. Stress, while having the potential to cause great damage to your mind, body and spirit is also an essential characteristic for strengthening our mental, physical and spiritual Self. Hence, it is beneficial for us to understand stress as an intrinsic life force of nature. A body builder cannot develop a muscular physique without adding "stress" or tension to the muscles in the body through constant repetition and the systematic application of pressure and weight. These active components are combined with the understanding of knowing how much rest to give the body during and after workouts so that the body has time to heal properly. Yet, in the same instance, an individual who overexerts his or herself by lifting too much weight before the body has developed enough strength and flexibility will bring harm to the body rather than make it stronger. A sculptured physique is the end result of learning how to practice self-discipline and how to be more generally in tune with the body.

There are numerous examples of the delicate balance that must be maintained within your daily life to promote growth and oppose deterioration. Sunlight, food and water are all vital to sustain our existence. At the same time, we need to maintain balance in regard to our intake and consumption. Balance ensures that equilibrium is maintained within the body thereby allowing us to perform at optimal levels.

The analogy of the body builder is also true within your mental and spiritual Self. For everything, there is a threshold at which there is over-consumption or under-consumption. While there must be an exertion of force for growth to occur, constant self-awareness must also be maintained from moment to moment in order to adequately address the dynamic flow of your mind, body and spirit. Your ultimate challenge in minimizing stress is learning to manage the shifts of mental, physical and spiritual energy that you experience in your everyday life. In many ways, effective stress management can be viewed as a balancing act defined by knowing how and when to replace the negative energy in your life with positive energy.

There are volumes of literature and scientific research on the causes and effects of stress. Most notable is Hans Selye, M.D. Through his scientific research of the causes of stress and the physical reactions of the body to stress, he developed the concept of the *general adaptation syndrome* (G.A.S.). This theory describes a process by which our bodies attempt to maintain homeostasis as we navigate and adjust to the constant changes that occur in and around us. Equally important, Selye supports the concept that stress is a natural part of life. In his classic book, *The Stress of Life* (1956), he states:

> No one can live without experiencing some degree of stress all the time. You may think that only serious disease or intensive physical or mental injury can cause stress. This is false. Crossing a busy intersection, exposure to a draft, or even sheer joy are enough to activate the body's stress mechanism to some extent. Stress is not even necessarily bad for you; it is also the spice of life, for any emotion, any activity causes stress. But, of course, your system must be prepared to take it. The same stress which makes one person sick can be an invigorating experience for another.
>
> It is through the *general adaptation syndrome*, or G.A.S., that our various internal organs – especially the endocrine glands and the nervous system – help us both to adjust to the constant changes which occur in and around us and to navigate a steady course toward whatever we consider a worthwhile goal (Selye, *The Stress of Life*, 1956, p. xv).

The *general adaptation syndrome* (GAS) is a predictable sequence of reactions that organisms show in response to stressors. This sequence consists of three stages: the Alarm stage, the Resistance stage, and the Exhaustion stage.

Stage I:

> **Alarm** – When there is emotional arousal and the defensive forces of the body are prepared to fight or flee.

Stage II:

> **Resistance** – When there are intense physiological efforts to either resist or adapt to the stressor.

Stage III:

> **Exhaustion** – Occurring if the organism fails in its efforts to resist the stressor.

The research of Richard Lazarus, another prominent expert, offers a perspective on stress that suggests, "it is not the stressor itself that causes stress, but a person's perception of the stressor" (Wood et al., 2004, p. 295). Consequently, in an effort to cope with various life stressors, individuals engage in a cognitive process of primary and secondary appraisals of life situations.

Primary Appraisal – an evaluation of the meaning and significance of the situation – whether its effect on one's well-being is positive, irrelevant, or negative.

There are potential outcomes of an individual appraising an event as stressful:

1. Harm or loss (damage that has already occurred)
2. Threat (the potential for harm or loss)
3. Challenge (the opportunity to grow or gain)

Secondary Appraisal – if people judge the situation to be within their control, they evaluate available resources:

- Physical (health, energy, stamina)
- Social (support network)
- Psychological (skills, morale, self-esteem)
- Material (money, tools, equipment)

> Wood et al., 2004, *Mastering the World of Psychology*, p. 295

The theories on stress by Selye and Lazarus, as noted above, have helped inform the holistic perspective applied in *The Self-Help Guide to Stress Management*. Foremost, the mental capacity of humans is recognized as a very powerful source for creating positive thoughts (as well as negative thoughts!) and for sustaining positive energy throughout our lives. Secondly, each concept is rooted in the belief that there is an ongoing interplay between mind, body and spirit in which we constantly perceive and interpret the events of our everyday lives. Most importantly, our ability to cope with life stressors is a reflection of the level (or degree) of self-awareness and self-understanding we have attained. Our personal level of these attributes is evidenced by our ability to consistently access available internal and external resources, as needed, to maintain a sense of balance and well-being. *The Self-Help Guide to Stress Management* seeks to integrate these concepts through a holistic framework. As such, this book can provide you with a comprehensive and systematic approach to develop the self-awareness, self-understanding and discipline necessary to 1) minimize the negative impact of stress and 2) achieve and maintain a greater sense of balance and well-being in your personal and professional lives.

Part I

10 STRATEGIES FOR EFFECTIVELY MANAGING STRESS

Mind

BALANCE & WELL-BEING

Body Spirit

Strategy Number 10:
Develop an Emergency Preparedness Plan in the Event of a Natural Disaster and/or Other Unexpected Environmental, National or Global Crisis

Strategy Number 9:
Financially Prepare for Economic Downturns, Job Layoffs, and/or Retirement

Strategy Number 8:
Be Consistent in Surrounding Yourself and Interacting with Positive People

Strategy Number 7:
Minimize Physical Clutter in Your Home and Workplace

Strategy Number 6:
Maintain Balance in Your Personal and professional lives by Identifying and Utilizing Tangible and Intangible Resources (Physical, Social, Psychological, Material)

Strategy Number 5:
Exercise Discipline in Working towards Large Goals by First Disciplining Yourself in Accomplishing Small Goals

Strategy Number 4:
Accept that Balance Can Be Achieved Only When There is an Equal Commitment to Your Mind, Body and Spirit

Strategy Number 3:
Be Honest with Yourself on a Daily Basis and in All Situations

Strategy Number 2:
Be Consistent in Setting Aside an Adequate Amount of Time to be Alone and in Silence (for Self-Reflection)

Strategy Number 1:
Accept that Stress Management is a Lifestyle that Requires You to be Proactive rather than Reactive

Strategy Number 1

Accept that Stress Management is a Lifestyle that Requires You to be Proactive Rather than Reactive

The Self-Help Guide to Stress Management

Stress
is a part
of Life
as we maneuver our way
through the demands
of work, play
and companionship —

such a delicate balance
we strive to attain.

But, once achieved,
it so easily
seems to
quietly slip away.

This is the dance
that we must Learn
to Love to Dance.

To constantly perceive
the near future
as one less fulfilling
if we fail
to do in this moment
what we know
must be done
to maintain balance in our lives.

                      Anthony Parnell

The desire to completely eliminate what we consider to be "bad" stress from our lives is not realistic. Stress will always be present in our personal and professional lives to some degree. Therefore, the shift in your thinking from "eliminating" stress to learning how to effectively "manage" stress creates a much broader range of possibilities once we begin to think in terms of implementing an effective stress management plan. This includes two essential components: 1) developing a written plan that lays out prioritized strategies that work best for you in helping to minimize stress and 2) sustaining consistency in performing activities in your daily life that promote well-being.

When we are committed to approaching each day as an opportunity to regain balance and to re-center ourselves, we gain an advantage for developing the discipline necessary to maintain a sense of balance and well-being. A person, however, can only minimize stress to the degree that they are committed to developing healthy habits in all key aspects of their daily life—mental and physical; personal and professional. Unfortunately, for many individuals, the concept of "process" is difficult to fully embrace as we have become conditioned to seek and to expect immediate answers and results to most things in life. Your ability, however, to maintain a healthy lifestyle that promotes balance and well-being is a step-by-step process that is not developed overnight. It requires a daily commitment to personal growth and maintaining balance despite the challenges and obstacles encountered in your personal and professional lives. In fully committing yourself to this process, you will over time, begin to develop new levels of discipline in your daily habits.

The Self-Help Guide to Stress Management

Personal Reflection on Strategy Number 1

24

Strategy Number 2

Be Consistent in Setting Aside an Adequate Amount of Time to be Alone and in Silence (for Self-Reflection)

The Self-Help Guide to Stress Management

Silence
is like water.

It is essential
to the body.

But, we usually
never get as much
of it
as we need....

Unless it becomes
a part of our
Daily Ritual
to Rise in Silence,
to Prepare Ourselves to Sleep
in Silence;

To take time
in the Middle of the day
to Rejuvenate Ourselves
with Silence & Meditation.

We, then, fail to become
that which we
once so greatly desired.

Anthony Parnell

Anthony Parnell, M.S.W.

The daily or regular ritual of being alone in silence, for writing or simply visualizing a balanced life, is required so as to constantly reinforce positive thinking and to maintain emotional equilibrium. We all require some degree of participation in activities that provide a healthy release for the buildup of negative energy. Granted, some individuals are able to maintain a high level of self-awareness and emotional balance without needing to adhere to a strict diet of daily mental and emotional exercises and rituals. However, for the vast majority of people, patience with oneself and a commitment to a holistic stress management plan are critical components of maintaining a balanced life.

For many individuals, the ability to embrace silence necessitates overcoming feelings of fear and discomfort with being alone. This can be a very difficult process for many because, over the years, we typically expend our time and energy avoiding a falsely perceived vulnerability with silence and stillness rather than embracing it to help us be in tune with our mind, body, and spirit. Or, we allow ourselves to become drowned by the demands and activities of our daily life which never seem to provide a sufficient opportunity for personal reflection and meditation.

You, then, have to make a purposeful effort to create opportunities for silence and time alone. The first step can be as simple as committing to *five minutes a day*. Then, you must determine a set time each day for your silence/alone time whether it is morning, afternoon or evening. Next is to determine where - either at home or at work (See Appendix). By committing to *five minutes a day* of silence and being alone, you create a starting point for learning how to take personal inventory, regularly and consistently. You will discover that in these sacred moments, you will instinctively begin to evaluate, assess and determine the adjustments that must be made in your personal and professional lives. You will also discover how calm you have become through your ability to unwind, relax and fully embrace the moment. And you may also realize just how anxious and imbalanced you have been by allowing your perpetual eagerness to always propel you on from one activity to the next.

The amount of silence and time needed to maintain a sense of balance and well-being varies with each individual. Only you can decide how much time alone, in silence, you actually need in order to maintain a sense of balance and well-being. What is most important is that you begin to understand that to adequately address your mental, physical and spiritual needs, you must make time to be alone in silence on a consistent, daily basis.

Anthony Parnell, M.S.W.

Personal Reflection on Strategy Number 2

Strategy Number 3

Be Honest with Yourself on a Daily Basis and in All Situations

The Self-Help Guide to Stress Management

The Truth
of who I am
remained a mystery...

until I no longer
could bear the disappointment,
the sadness
of finding myself
in the same emotional
and physical rut—
time and time again.

I finally said to myself
that I truly am ready
for change,
lasting change . . .

And, then,
the realest,
truest parts
of who I am
were shadows no longer.

                    Anthony Parnell

Honesty with yourself is essential because life's demands take their toll on our mental, physical and spiritual well-being. Because stress is a part of life, adjustments have to be made to maintain a sense of balance, personally and professionally. However, adjustments cannot be made if you do not possess a level of self-awareness that will enable you to respond accordingly to specific challenges as they arise.

Learning to be honest with yourself goes hand in hand with learning to effectively cope with life situations. This includes accepting personal limitations. You cannot be all things to all people. You cannot be all places at once. You cannot be friends with everyone. Ultimately, as you become more honest with yourself, your ability to effectively cope with life situations becomes contingent on two interrelated sub-strategies: 1) doing everything within your power to help yourself, and 2) remaining open to giving and receiving emotional support from others.

The Self-Help Guide to Stress Management

Personal Reflection on Strategy Number 3

Strategy Number 4

Accept that Balance Can be Achieved Only When There is an Equal Commitment to One's Mind, Body and Spirit

The Self-Help Guide to Stress Management

"The Balance of One"

The Mind.

The Body.

The Spirit

are One.

Each
as intricately connected
to the other
as branches on a tree.

Though much more
than the physical make-up
of my being,

and much more
than pure intellect,

it is my spiritual nature
that provides the roots
of my existence.

I, then, must continuously nourish
All Elements of who I am
to maintain the continuity
of the Oneness
of my being.

Anthony Parnell

There is an inherent harmony that exists between mind, body and spirit. For this reason, *The Self-Help Guide to Stress Management* is rooted in the philosophy that balance and well-being can only be achieved and maintained when the needs of your mind, body and spirit are adequately and equally addressed. It is also necessary for us to understand that a holistic perspective of balance and well-being means that we take into account both our internal and external conditions. This is because your physical, mental and spiritual states of existence are interconnected.

It also requires us to understand and accept that a holistic perspective of balance and well-being is representative of our internal as well as external condition. Thus, your physical condition should not be given greater emphasis than your mental or spiritual condition as an indicator of health, balance and well-being. The same is true of individuals who focus exclusively or primarily on achieving balance in their professional lives but neglect their personal lives.

As you adopt new beliefs about the holistic connection between mind, body, and spirit, you are likely to be more compelled to explore all aspects of your multi-dimensionality. You may begin to see a deeper purpose and meaning to our existence that extends beyond simply accumulating material possessions and defining ourselves by our social status. *The Self-Help Guide to Stress Management* offers both philosophical and practical guidance to help you begin to make that shift towards a more holistic thought process and holistic approach to minimizing stress in your personal and professional lives.

The Self-Help Guide to Stress Management

Personal Reflection on Strategy Number 4

Strategy Number 5:

Exercise Discipline in Working towards Large Goals by First Disciplining Yourself in Accomplishing Small Goals

The Self-Help Guide to Stress Management

I move toward my goal
as time has become my ally
rather than my foe.

I understand that
where I want to be tomorrow
begins with what I do today.

My sense of success
is measured mostly
by having positive feelings
about who I am as a person
and learning to accept myself
for where I am
at this stage of my Life.

Because I have let go
of my disappointments
and failures of the past,
I can set realistic goals
for my future.

                          Anthony Parnell

Setting goals is a fundamental part of life. They can serve as a motivational tool and provide a sense of direction in any given area. However, most individuals have not developed the combined habits of first writing goals and then following up by reviewing them periodically.

Step-by-Step Goals is an approach I offer for creating goals that you can apply to your personal and professional lives. The goals you create may be directed toward virtually any area of your life that include (but are not limited to) your spiritual, mental/psychological, physical, financial, and career-related activities. I refer to these goals as Step-by-Step Goals because the emphasis of the exercise is placed on outlining how one can accomplish his or her goals in small incremental 'steps' within given timelines (Later, Part II, when discussing "Developing Prioritized Stress Management Goals," I will provide several examples of Step-by-Step Goals).

The greatest benefit of practicing Step-by-Step Goals is that you are able to focus on moving forward in a way that is most comfortable for you; that is, accomplishing your long-term goals over a reasonable time as opposed to placing too much emphasis on accomplishing your "ultimate" goal all at once. In other words, Step-by-Step Goals force you to take small steps and to be patient as we begin to focus on our growth and development one day at a time. A second benefit is that, by establishing increments, you are more inclined to set realistic goals. This is true because short-term goals help to give us more objectivity in regard to what we need to do each day in order to achieve our long-term goals.

The Self-Help Guide to Stress Management

A final benefit is that you can feel a more immediate sense of accomplishment. This comes from more frequent opportunities to reward ourselves as we successfully complete each milestone. For some, this slight adjustment in how you approach your stress management goal-setting will be essential for maintaining high levels of motivation.

Anthony Parnell, M.S.W.

Personal Reflection on Strategy Number 5

Strategy Number 6

Maintain Balance in Your Personal and professional lives by Identifying, Utilizing and/or Creating Tangible and Intangible Resources (Physical, Social, Psychological, Spiritual, Material)

The Self-Help Guide to Stress Management

I Am My Greatest Resource
because
I Am Resilient.

I Am My Greatest Resource
because
I Am Creative.

I Am My Greatest Resource
because
I am not afraid,
or too prideful,
to Ask for Help
when Needed.

                        Anthony Parnell

Anthony Parnell, M.S.W.

During my freshman year of college, I was inspired to take the initiative to create a resource that wasn't available. As many of us know, the college experience leaves us to fend for ourselves in taking responsibility for learning healthy definitions of adulthood, which for me was manhood. I started a Men's Group for male students to discuss how they define and express their manhood. It wasn't until years later that I realized the overarching significance of creating the group: at first, we don't always see exactly what to do in addressing the ever-changing needs of our mind, body and spirit. But, if we listen to our "inner voice" and aren't afraid to try different things, we may just find – or in my case, create - the tangible or intangible resource we need at that particular moment in our life.

In other instances, the exact internal or external resource we need is right in front of us. We just have to be motivated and disciplined enough to utilize it. Take for example a patient who goes to the doctor for a routine checkup only to discover that their cholesterol and blood sugar are too high and they are twenty pounds overweight. Even more, they have been informed by their physician that, if they don't change their diet and lose at least twenty pounds, they are in danger of having a heart attack or a stroke. At a minimum, some of the resources readily available to address these health challenges are 1) hire a personal trainer, 2) signup for a gym membership, or 3) hire a personal chef or dietician. He or she might even purchase a watch or device that will track the number of calories they burn each day.

The Self-Help Guide to Stress Management

Personal Reflection on Strategy Number 6

Strategy Number 7

Minimize Physical Clutter in Your Home and Workplace

The Self-Help Guide to Stress Management

Decluttering one's physical environment can immediately make one feel lighter.

But, just as it is recommended to begin with 5 Minutes a Day of Writing and Self-Reflection, the same is true of Decluttering one's Physical Environment.

Begin with small steps to ensure consistency and forward progress.

Anthony Parnell

The negative impact that Physical Clutter has on an individual varies from person to person. For some, it's a minor distraction that they are able to easily tune out. For others, it drives them crazy! They just can't get any work done when the dishes are not clean, when there's clothes on the floor or there's piles of paper on their desk.

The most important thing in consistently managing physical clutter in your home and work environment is to maintain self-awareness of the impact it's having on your stress levels. In other words, know your personal limits. Ask yourself: What degree of organization do I need in my physical environment for me to be able to concentrate, focus and function at my highest level?

If you determine that the physical clutter in your life is contributing to higher stress levels, there's a number of things you can do to begin removing the clutter. The first step is to just get started doing something in the way of decluttering. For example, pick a particular room or section of a room that you know needs attention. Even giving 15-30 minutes the first day can make a difference. Then, you can gradually increase the amount of time you spend decluttering {Refer to Appendix for a more detailed approach to tackling physical clutter in your home or workplace}.

The Self-Help Guide to Stress Management

Personal Reflection on Strategy Number 7

Strategy Number 8

Be Consistent in Surrounding Yourself and Interacting with Positive People

"True friends always wish the best for us."

Anthony Parnell

~

The Self-Help Guide to Stress Management

Friendship Rule to Live By

If you call someone Your
Friend,
you should be able to have
PEACE OF MIND
about anything
they say or do.

Anthony Parnell

Anthony Parnell, M.S.W.

The people we interact with on a daily basis are either giving us energy or taking energy from us. Thus, in the pursuit of our stress management goals, two of the biggest responsibilities are 1) maintaining a heightened sense of awareness of our current needs - emotionally and spiritually – and, 2) monitoring whether or not the individuals we interact with regularly are giving us the kind of positive energy we need. The more time we spend with individuals who habitually exercise negative thinking and negative behavior, the more difficult it is for us to maintain a sense of balance and well-being.

Living our lives in total isolation, however, is not the answer. The reality is that we all experience moments when we need a solid support system to call upon and lean on. Therefore, it is critically important to ensure that we have an adequate support system around us to help us navigate through life's challenges. In addition to trying our best to maintain healthy, loving and fulfilling relationships with our families and friends, it is also important that we do not limit ourselves. We must be proactive in our efforts to expand our support system, both personally and professionally. To this end, we should actively seek out appropriate mentors, prayer partners and/or social groups that we can join or create—people with whom the exchange of nurturing, positive energy is mutual and reciprocal (See Appendix for additional tools).

The Self-Help Guide to Stress Management

Personal Reflection on Strategy Number 8

Strategy Number 9

Financially Prepare for Economic Downturns, Job Layoffs, and/or Retirement

The Self-Help Guide to Stress Management

Each Day that I rise
is another day
that I move closer
to being all that I was meant
to be.

While I have learned
to be patient with the process
of becoming a greater me,
I now Understand
that learning to maintain
Uncluttered Thoughts and Emotions,
an Uncluttered Environment,
and Uncluttered Finances
are critical steps in learning
to exercise the discipline required
to maintain balance and well-being
in my daily life.

Anthony Parnell

The world of finance is saturated with experts on financial health. Each one offers us ways on how best to prepare ourselves for economic downturns, job layoffs and retirement. One of the most profound concepts I have encountered for making sound financial decisions and assessing financial health is found in Suze Orman's book, *The Laws of Money (2004),* which represents a basic philosophy of money management and financial decision-making that I have found to be simple, easy to understand, and applicable to individuals from all income levels.

Orman's 5 Laws of Money

Law #1: Truth Creates Money, Lies Destroy It

Law #2: Look at What You Have, Not at What You Had

Law #3: Do What is Right for You, Before You Do What Is Right for Your Money

Law #4: Invest in the Known Before the Unknown

Law #5: Always Remember: Money Has No Power of Its Own

As you begin to implement the other nine strategies for effectively managing stress, I urge you to take some time to make a list of some specific things you can do that will move you in the direction of creating more financial security for yourself. Some you can do immediately. Others will require patience and several steps to accomplish over an extended period of time.

The Self-Help Guide to Stress Management

Things You Can Do Now to become Financially Stronger

1. Open a Savings Account

2. Start Saving a minimum of $50 per Paycheck

3. Look for Part-Time Work opportunities to create additional Discretionary Income and Savings

4. Explore and Write Down possible Ideas for starting a Part-Time Homebased Business

5. Take Inventory of All of your Personal Belongings to see what Items can be Sold to Create some Initial or Additional Savings

6. Attend a "Free" Credit Repair Workshop/Seminar in your local community (Or, Watch "Free" Credit Repair Courses on YouTube)

Anthony Parnell, M.S.W.

Personal Reflection on Strategy Number 9

Strategy Number 10

Develop an Emergency Preparedness Plan in the Event of a Natural Disaster and/or Other Unexpected Environmental, National or Global Crisis

The Self-Help Guide to Stress Management

Sometimes,
motivation must come
solely from within.

Sometimes,
there is
no other inspiration
except our intense desire,
a deep yearning
for much more
to be revealed
about the essence
of who we really are;

and to feel a sense of peace
and clarity
about the meaning
and the quality
of our lives.

                    Anthony Parnell

Anthony Parnell, M.S.W.

Many individuals have a difficult time contemplating the thought of a loved one passing. Global crises and increasing environmental concerns, however, are forcing more and more Americans and all citizens of the world to come to terms with the fragility of life. As I expressed earlier in the book, stress is a natural part of life for which we can proactively take steps to manage. The same can be said in regard to having an Emergency Preparedness Plan ready to use in the event of a natural disaster or other unexpected crisis.

When we look at major disasters that have occurred in the United States and globally over the past 20 years, it is a reminder that crises are inevitable. We, therefore, can use the present moment to begin planning ahead. We can choose to take a proactive stance toward empowering ourselves to be as prepared as we possibly can be for any unforeseen disaster.

Even if you don't elect to take comprehensive measures in developing and implementing an Emergency Preparedness Plan, here is a list of some of the things you might consider:

A Will	Candles and Lighters
A Living Trust	Power Generator
A Durable Power of Attorney	Gallons of Gasoline for your Car
Life Insurance Policy	Face Masks
Emergency Savings	Blankets
Bottled Water Supply	Portable Heater
Non-Perishable Food Items	

The Self-Help Guide to Stress Management

A Sample of some of the U.S. Crises and Natural Disasters in the Last 20 Years	A Sample of some of the Global Crises and Natural Disasters in the Last 20 Years
COVID-19 Pandemic Hurricanes (Katrina, Sandy, Maria) Rise in Mass Shootings 9/11 (September 11, 2001) Western Wildfires, California Firestorm	COVID-19 Pandemic 2008 Economic Crisis Terrorism Earthquakes Tsunamis

SOURCE:
Our World in Data (ourworldindata.org)

Anthony Parnell, M.S.W.

Personal Reflection on Strategy Number 10

> The Self-Help Guide to Stress Management

STOP!

Now that you have been introduced to the "10 Strategies for Effectively Managing Stress," I would like you to take some time to think about how consistently you practice and how strongly you believe in each of these strategies.

As a first step, review and complete the **STRESS MANAGEMENT REPORT CARD (Self-Graded)** on the following page. Give yourself a grade in each of the ten strategies. (A = highest score; F = lowest score)

> **A = Very Strong** I do an amazing job of using this Strategy regularly in my life.
>
> **B = Strong** I do a good job of using this Strategy in my life.
>
> **C = Average** I have used this Strategy a few times but still need to work on using it more.
>
> **D = Okay** I only remember using this Strategy once or twice in my life.
>
> **F = Needs a Lot of Work** I do not remember ever using this Strategy in my life.

Remember, there are no right or wrong answers. The self-graded report card simply serves as a measuring stick of how you currently view yourself in relation to the Ten Strategies. Once you've completed the Self-Graded Report Card, it will be much easier to pinpoint which strategies you might want to prioritize and give the greatest amount of attention.

As a second step, you are encouraged to record any general thoughts and/or observations of how you see your life at this time. Also, consider 1) Are you currently using these strategies in your life? 2) If so, in what ways can they begin to have a greater impact in your life? That is, how can they become a stronger influence in your life? Space for writing is provided on the page following the Report Card.

The Self-Help Guide to Stress Management

10 Strategies for Effectively Managing Stress

STRESS MANAGEMENT REPORT CARD (Self-Graded)	
ELEMENTS	**GRADE**
Strategy Number 1: Accept that Stress Management is a Lifestyle that Requires an Individual to be Proactive rather than Reactive	
Strategy Number 2: Be Consistent in Setting Aside an Adequate Amount of Time to be Alone and in Silence (for Self-Reflection)	
Strategy Number 3: Be Honest with Yourself on a Daily Basis and in All Situations	
Strategy Number 4: Accept that Balance Can Be Achieved Only When There is an Equal Commitment to Your Mind, Body and Spirit	
Strategy Number 5: Exercise Discipline in Working towards Large Goals By First Disciplining Yourself in Accomplishing Small Goals	
Strategy Number 6: Maintain Balance in Your Personal and professional lives by Identifying and Utilizing Tangible and Intangible Resources (Physical, Social, Psychological, Material)	
Strategy Number 7: Minimize Physical Clutter in Your Home and Workplace	
Strategy Number 8: Be Consistent in Surrounding Yourself and Interacting with Positive People	
Strategy Number 9: Financially Prepare for Economic Downturns, Job Layoffs, and/or Retirement	
Strategy Number 10: Develop an Emergency Preparedness Plan in the Event of a Natural Disaster and/or Other Unexpected Environmental, National or Global Crisis	

Anthony Parnell, M.S.W.

Personal Reflection on the Self-Graded "Stress Management" Report Card

Part II

APPLYING THE "10 STRATEGIES" TO EVERYDAY LIFE

The Self-Help Guide to Stress Management

In Part I, I laid a solid foundation for you to effectively manage stress in your personal and professional lives. Here in Part II, I want to provide you with an opportunity to practice utilizing and incorporating the "10 Strategies" into your daily life. This includes writing clear stress management goals, prioritizing those goals and identifying internal and external resources that will aid you in accomplishing them. This is critical because when your stress level is high it can be difficult to know where to focus your attention in your efforts to minimize your stress. As emphasized throughout this book, stress is a part of life. By having a stress management plan in place, you are being proactive in your efforts to maintain balance and well-being in both the personal and professional areas of your life.

To help you begin implementing the "10 Strategies for Effectively Managing Stress" into your daily routine, there's a series of steps I will walk you through. For example, the first step is simply to reemphasize the importance of setting aside a minimum of *5 Minutes a Day* for writing and self-reflection. Self-awareness and a willingness to be honest with yourself are the two most essential building blocks for managing stress. I firmly believe that without practicing these strategies, you will not be able to consistently identify and address the needs of your mind, body, spirit or successfully manage the many other challenges that will inevitably descend upon you in your daily life.

Anthony Parnell, M.S.W.

STEPS TO APPLYING THE "10 STRATEGIES"

Step Number 5
Putting It All Together
(Maintaining an Effective Stress Management Plan)

Step Number 4
Identify Internal & External Resources

Step Number 3
Develop Prioritized Stress Management Goals

Step Number 2
Identify Warning Signs & Stressors

Step Number 1
Maintain a Commitment to "5 Minutes a Day" of Writing and Self-Reflection

Step Number 1:

Maintain a Commitment to "5 Minutes a Day" of Writing and Self-Reflection (Maintain Decluttered Thoughts and Emotions)

The stress we experience in daily life frequently comes from feeling that current circumstances are unmanageable. Yet, in an instant, the simple practice of decluttering your thoughts and emotions can help you transition to a mood of light-heartedness and a sense of greater empowerment. This transition can be accomplished by writing your thoughts and expressing emotions in a journal or notebook as well as talking to friends.

The Self-Help Guide to Stress Management

Unfortunately, if your energy has been drained by increasing demands placed on your time and energy, it can become more and more challenging to remove the emotional clutter in your life. Thus, I encourage you to make writing a part of your daily life. As shared earlier, the book *Healing through Writing* discusses this method in depth and provides specific examples on how writing can be utilized as a tool to empower you by preventing the build-up of negative energy and emotions and to facilitate personal growth.

The ability to exercise discipline in your commitment to writing daily, or on a consistent basis, can take time to develop. Writing requires effort, focus, and discipline. Therefore, you are encouraged to begin with an initial commitment of five minutes a day for five consecutive days. This period of five minutes should be a free-flowing experience in which you record any thoughts and emotions that you become aware of, whether the thoughts and ideas can be recorded clearly or not. Selecting a time of day that you feel would be conducive to writing is also important. If you experience difficulty getting started or in maintaining a consistent flow, "Six Steps To Picking Up the Pen," taken from *Healing through Writing*, is presented below to assist you in relaxing and focusing your writing. This is followed by a chart you can use to record your daily efforts to write for *Five Minutes A Day for Five Consecutive Days!*

Six Steps to Picking Up the Pen

1. Set a Time

Select a time of day that is best for you to concentrate and focus your energy (morning, afternoon, after dinner, before bed, and so on). This is a time that you feel would be most conducive for you to write. My mind is most clear early in the morning or late at night. Whatever time you choose, make sure you take a moment or two to unwind and transition from your previous activity. For instance, instead of trying to immediately write, take a few moments to pause and reflect on any recent progress you've made. This may prove beneficial in creating a sense of organization to your thoughts and emotions.

2. Choose a Comfortable Location to Write

Think of a relaxing environment in which you are not likely to be interrupted or distracted. Also, consider a location in your home or office where you feel the greatest sense of peace or positive energy.

3. Set the Mood with Music

Once you have set a time and located a comfortable, relaxing environment, you will have to determine whether a certain style of music will be helpful to set the mood. It is important that both your mind and body are calm and relaxed, enabling you to channel your energy and focus on your inner self. For most beginners, music will be necessary to help them sustain their focus. Even after years of practice and experience, there still are times when it is extremely difficult for me to identify or express my intense emotions without the aid of some music that resonates with my mood. The right music setting the right mood helps me to relax and become more open to my thoughts and emotions. With practice and time, you too will be able to identify the source of your emotions and freely express them.

4. Focus on Breathing

Sit with your legs folded, close your eyes, and take long, slow, deep breaths to relax your body and clear your mind. As you breathe, inhale through your nose and exhale through your mouth. When inhaling, focus on taking in positive energy and filling your lungs and chest with air. While slowly exhaling, focus on releasing negative energy and negative thoughts. Be careful of the pace of your breathing so as to not become dizzy. Then ask yourself, "How do I feel?" as you continue taking long, slow deep breaths and gradually become content with silence and stillness. You should now feel completely relaxed, with no tension in your shoulders. And, your arms and hands should be comfortably resting at your side.

5. Write Your Real Emotions

Release expectations of others and the urge to judge what you write about your emotions. In learning to accept your emotions *and your writing*, you are learning to accept yourself and where you are in your process of spiritual growth and self-awareness.

6. Take Small Steps

On a daily basis, celebrate each accomplishment. Congratulate yourself for having the discipline to write, even if only for five minutes. Focus on consistency and detail. Remember: With time and practice you will develop the ability to honestly and succinctly express your thoughts and emotions through the healthy medium of writing.

It is now time to make a commitment to write in your journal or to sit in silence/meditation for five minutes a day for five consecutive days. Use the following chart to record your progress. Additional tracking charts are provided in the Appendix.

Sample Tracking Log
for Decluttering Thoughts and Emotions

DAY OF THE WEEK	AMOUNT OF TIME
DAY 1	2 MINUTES
DAY 2	2 MINUTES
DAY 3	NO ENTRY
DAY 4	6 MINUTES
DAY 5	10 MINUTES

Reader's Chart
for Tracking Decluttering Thoughts and Emotions

DAY OF THE WEEK	AMOUNT OF TIME
DAY 1	
DAY 2	
DAY 3	
DAY 4	
DAY 5	

Step Number 2:

Identify Warning Signs & Stressors

As shared with you in the Introduction to this book when providing "A Basic Understanding of Stress," everyone responds differently to stress. So, the greater degree of self-awareness you possess the more equipped you will be to minimize the negative effects of stress. Here in Step Number 2, I would like you to take some time to assess your current level of self-awareness by identifying warning signs and stressors. Warning Signs are "physical, emotional, behavioral and cognitive indicators of the negative impact of stress." Stressors can be defined as "that which produces stress" (Selye, 1956, p. 78). Stressors can range from illness and environmental factors to financial concerns or starting a new job.

The identification of Warning Signs and Stressors can serve as a starting point (and subsequently a barometer) for gauging the fluctuations in your stress levels. Therefore, identifying Warning Signs and Stressors is critical, in that it challenges you to begin to develop a proactive strategy for stress management. Equally, it will challenge you to expand your self-awareness to the degree that will enable you to maintain a sustainable balance in your personal and professional lives.

It is also critical to identify the Warning Sign as early as possible. The earlier you detect an imbalance, the sooner balance can be restored to your mind, body, and spirit. Failure to identify warning signs of stress in its early stages has long-term implications for your mental and physical well-being. According to the National Institute for Occupational Safety and Health,

". . . Evidence is rapidly accumulating to suggest that stress plays an important role in several types of chronic health problems especially...

- Cardiovascular Disease (coronary heart disease, stroke, hypertensive heart disease),

- Musculoskeletal Disorders (job stress increases the risk of back disorders),

- Psychological Disorders (mental health problems such as depression and burnout)."

National Institute for Occupational and Safety and Health (1999), *Stress at work* (pages 10–11)

Anthony Parnell, M.S.W.

A brief list of employment and non-employment-related Warning Signs are listed on the following page. **Take a few moments to circle and then record any Warning Signs** that you can immediately identify. Feel free to add to the list any additional Warning Signs or Symptoms that you are able to identify in your personal or professional life.

The Self-Help Guide to Stress Management

Early Warning Signs of Job Stress (NIOSH *Stress at Work* Publication 99-101, page 11)

Headache

Sleep Disturbances

Difficulty in Concentrating

Short Temper

Upset Stomach

Job Dissatisfaction

Low Morale

Examples of Other Early Warning Signs (Physical, Mental, Emotional, Behavioral)

Irritability

Sleeping Too Much or Too Little

Exhaustion

Weight Gain or Loss

General Aches and Pains

Increased Use of Alcohol or Drugs

Memory Problems

Inability to Relax

Feeling Overwhelmed

Anthony Parnell, M.S.W.

Reader's List:
Write any Warning Signs you recognize from your Personal and Professional lives

1.

2.

3.

4.

5.

6.

7.

IDENTIFYING STRESSORS

Now that you have identified some of the warning signs of stress, you now need to clearly identify and name your current personal and professional stressors.

A host of environmental and social causative factors can take a toll on your mind, body, and spirit. With regards to a work environment, NIOSH identifies six conditions that may lead to job stress:

1. The Design of Task
2. Management Style
3. Interpersonal Relationships
4. Work Roles
5. Career Concerns
6. Environmental Conditions

> National Institute for Occupational and Safety and Health (1999), *Stress at work* (page 9)

The National Institute for Occupational Safety and Health also reports that effectively managing stress in one's work environment requires an active role for the individual as well as the employer. Working in a professional environment that makes a conscious effort to address the emotional needs of workers is essential to minimizing the negative impact of stress. Given that, "Problems at work are more strongly associated with health complaints than any other life stressor – more so than even financial problems or family problems . . .", the management of organizations can play a vital role in stress prevention in the workplace and an increased sense of balance and well-being among countless individuals (*Stress At Work,* page 5).

Changes within any organization that are needed to prevent job stress include:

- Ensuring that the workload is in line with workers' capabilities and resources.

- Designing jobs to provide meaning, stimulation, and opportunities for workers to use their skills.

- Clearly defining workers' roles and responsibilities.

- Giving workers opportunities to participate in decisions and actions affecting their jobs.

- Improving communication – reduce uncertainty about career development and future employment prospects.

- Providing opportunities for social interaction among workers.

- Establishing work schedules that are compatible with demands and responsibilities outside the job.

The emphasis of this book is to empower you to make the necessary adjustments within your personal life and professional environment to maintain a sense of balance and well-being. This includes developing the ability to effectively manage stress with or without ideal support being available from an employer. However, for employers who are committed to reducing employee stress, additional tools are available in the Appendix and "Additional Resources" section at the end of this book.

To complete Step Number 2, several common stressors are **listed below**. Upon reviewing the lists of stressors, **circle and then record any stressors** you recognize from your professional life. If needed, refer to answers from the Self-Exploratory Questions in Appendix A and "Personal Reflections" on any of the "10 Strategies" in Part I.

Job Stressors (NIOSH *Stress At Work Publication No. 99-101*, page 9)

The Design of Task

Management Style

Interpersonal Relationships

Work Roles

Career Concerns

Environmental Conditions

~

Other Common Stressors

Money

Health/Illness

Relationships

Relocation

Legal Problems

Reader's List:

Write the Stressors you recognize from your Personal and professional lives

1.

2.

3.

4.

5.

6.

7.

The Self-Help Guide to Stress Management

Now, prioritize the list of stressors according to those that have the greatest negative impact on your personal and/or professional life (#1, #2, #3 and so on).

Sample Prioritized List of Stressors:

1. Long Hours and Workload
2. Clutter at Home
3. Clutter at Office
4. Limited/Minimal Task Variety in Work Environment
5. Limited Intellectual and Spiritual Stimulation
6. Limited time alone to write, read and reflect/meditate
7. Inadequate Amounts of Exercise
8. Inadequate Amounts of Sleep (staying up late writing)

Reader's Prioritized List of Stressors:

1.
2.
3.
4.
5.
6.
7.
8.

Once again, the impact of stressors varies from individual to individual. And, as previously noted, developing self-awareness is the key to regularly monitoring the positive and negative impact of stress in your life. There are also numerous tools for measuring stress levels and common indicators such as cholesterol and blood pressure levels. It is strongly recommended that physicians or health professionals be consulted in addition to incorporating the philosophy and techniques offered here in *The Self-Help Guide to Stress Management*. Further, if you are experiencing extreme difficulty performing normal tasks or coping with situations at home or work, it is strongly recommended that a mental health professional be consulted. The "Additional Resources" section of this book provides professional referral information as well as sources for more detailed information on stress and other health related questions.

Step Number 3:

Develop Prioritized Stress Management Goals

Your may already participate in regular extracurricular and leisure activities to maintain a sense of balance and to minimize stress. Healthy activities, exercises and hobbies are valuable resources for minimizing stress in your personal and professional lives. The reason why is simple: you find them fun and relaxing! Rather than taking energy from you, these activities energize you. It is important to first identify extracurricular and leisure activities that energize you, before incorporating your stressors and warning signs (identified and recorded in Step Number 2) into a formal stress management plan.

Take a few moments to list any important extracurricular or leisure activities that you believe are beneficial for minimizing stress in your personal and professional lives.

The Self-Help Guide to Stress Management

Here are some examples you might include in your list:

> Playing basketball;
>
> Watching NBA basketball;
>
> Reading biographies on the lives of great people;
>
> Watching interviews or biographies of prominent entertainers, musicians, actors, businessmen and political figures;
>
> Watching standup comedians;
>
> Watching nature shows;
>
> Spending time at the ocean or near water;
>
> Traveling;
>
> Massage Therapy;
>
> Live Entertainment (Music, Dance, Theater)

I. Reader's Quick List of Preferred Extracurricular and Leisure Activities:

_____

_____

_____

_____

_____

_____

II. Now consider which activities are the most enjoyable and the most effective in minimizing stress and the buildup of negative energy in your personal and professional lives. Prioritize your list of Extracurricular and Leisure Activities (numbering #1, #2, #3 and so on).

A Sample List of Prioritized Stress Deterrents:

1. Spending Time Alone in Silence (meditating or journaling/writing)
2. Engaging in deeply intellectual conversations about spirituality or life in general
3. Playing basketball
4. Watching NBA basketball
5. Spending time at the ocean or near water
6. Watching Live Entertainment
7. Massage Therapy
8. Watching stand-up comedy acts
9. Watching interviews or biographies of prominent entertainers, musicians, actors, businessmen, political figures
10. Watching great drama/suspense films
11. Traveling to other cities and countries
12. Reading biographies on the lives of great people
13. Playing piano and writing music
14. Watching nature shows

The Self-Help Guide to Stress Management

Reader's Prioritized Stress Deterrents:

1.
2.
3.
4.
5.
6.
7.
8.
9.
10.
11.
12.
13.
14.

III. Ask yourself how much time you need to engage in each of these activities on a regular basis in order to feel a sense of balance and to minimize stress. A chart to record the results has been provided **below**. The Appendix provides additional charts for tracking your progress in incorporating extracurricular and leisure activities into your daily lifestyle.

Sample Extracurricular Activity Chart

	ACTIVITY	MINIMUM AMOUNT OF TIME NEEDED TO MAINTAIN BALANCE
1.	Spending Time Alone in Silence (meditating or journaling)	1 hour a day
2.	Engaging in deeply intellectual conversations about spirituality or life in general	1-3 hours per day (6-8 hours a week)
3.	Playing basketball	2-3 days per week for at least 1 hour a day
4.	Watching NBA Basketball	1 or 2 games per week
5.	Spending time alone at the ocean or near the water	1 day per month

The Self-Help Guide to Stress Management

	ACTIVITY	MINIMUM AMOUNT OF TIME NEEDED TO MAINTAIN BALANCE
6.	Watching Live Entertainment	At least 1 Show every two weeks
7.	Massage Therapy	1-2 times per month
8.	Watching stand-up comedy acts or comedy shows/ comedy series	2 hours per week
9.	Watching interviews or biographies on television of prominent entertainers, musicians, actors, businessmen, political figures	4 hours per week
10.	Watching great drama/ suspense films	2 hours per week
11.	Traveling	A 3-day weekend out of town every other month; a minimum of 1-2 full weeks a year
12.	Reading biographies on the lives of great people	1 book every 3-6 months
13.	Playing piano and writing music	4 hours per week
14.	Watching nature shows	2 hours per week

Anthony Parnell, M.S.W.

Reader's Extracurricular Activity Chart

ACTIVITY	MINIMUM AMOUNT OF TIME NEEDED TO MAINTAIN BALANCE
1.	
2.	
3.	
4.	
5.	
6.	
7.	
8.	
9.	
10.	
11.	
12.	
13.	
14.	

Thus far you have: 1) identified and prioritized the primary stressors in your personal and professional lives; and, 2) determined extracurricular and leisure activities that can help in minimizing the negative impact of stress. Now you are ready to begin the process of developing specific, concise stress management goals related to each primary stressor. This will be accomplished by writing an "I will . . . " statement for each of the three primary stressors.

As a visual reminder, list your three primary stressors from Step Number 2.

For example:

1. Long Hours and Workload
2. Clutter at Home
3. Clutter at Office

Select any of your three primary stressors to begin writing your first Goal Statement. Repeat for the other two primary stressors. Then, after writing a Goal Statement for each of the three primary stressors, prioritize the goal statements (#1, #2, #3 and so on).

Helpful hint: Your first instinct may be to select the greatest stressor for recording Goal Statement #1. However, in many instances, your initial emphasis should be placed on the goal statement that is *easiest to accomplish*. As emphasized with Step-by-Step Goals in Strategy #5, the reason for this recommended strategy is to support your effort toward feeling an immediate sense of accomplishment and to avoid feeling defeated because of difficulty or inability to make progress in accomplishing a goal.

When writing an "I will ..." goal statement, focus on connecting each of the stressors with one of your recorded Leisure/Extracurricular Activities. Think about what activity you feel will adequately counteract or neutralize the negative impact of the stressor.

Sample entry:

> Primary Stressor #1: Long Hours at Work and Workload
>
> Goal Statement #1: I will reduce the numbers of hours I work per week by staying at work no later than 7pm or 8pm every night and by leaving work at 4pm at least one day a week to play basketball for a minimum of 1 hour (I also will play basketball for at least one hour on Saturday or Sunday).
>
> An Alternative Goal Statement #1: I will jog for 30 minutes Mondays and Thursdays at 6am before going to work to ensure that I have an outlet for releasing aggression and tension that builds up from working long hours at work.

The process continues through your list. Record a Goal Statement for Prioritized Stressor #2, then #3. It is recommended to begin by recording a maximum of three goal statements. No more than one goal statement should be implemented per week. Once you have developed the discipline to incorporate your first three prioritized goals into your daily lifestyle, then additional goal statements can be added (see Appendix F).

The Self-Help Guide to Stress Management

The following examples are given to help you implement your Stress Management Goals:

Primary Stressor #1: Long Hours at Work and Workload

Goal Statement #1: I will reduce the numbers of hours I work per week by staying at work no later than 7pm or 8pm every night and by leaving work at 4pm at least one day a week to play basketball for a minimum of 1 hour (I also will play basketball for at least one hour on Saturday or Sunday).

~

Primary Stressor #2: Clutter at Home

Goal Statement #2: I will schedule Saturday mornings at 11am as my weekly time

to declutter my office space at home.

~

Primary Stressor #3: Clutter in Office

Goal Statement #3: I will schedule Monday mornings at 8am and Thursday mornings at 8am as my weekly times to declutter my office at work.

Anthony Parnell, M.S.W.

Sample Stress Management Goals Chart

WEEK #1

GOAL #1:

I will reduce the numbers of hours I work per week by staying at work no later than 7pm or 8pm every night and by leaving work at 4pm at least one day a week to play basketball for a minimum of 1 hour (I will also play basketball for at least one hour on Saturday or Sunday).

	MON	TUE	WED	THU	FRI	SAT	SUN
GOAL #1:	4pm I Left early to play basketball					I Played Basketball	

WEEK #2

GOAL #1:

I will reduce the numbers of hours I work per week by staying at work no later than 7pm or 8pm every night and by leaving work at 4pm at least one day a week to play basketball for a minimum of 1 hour (I will also play basketball for at least one hour on Saturday or Sunday).

GOAL #2:

I will schedule Saturday mornings at 11am as my weekly time to declutter my office space at home.

The Self-Help Guide to Stress Management

	MON	TUE	WED	THU	FRI	SAT	SUN
GOAL #1:			4pm I Left early to play basketball			I Played Basketball	
GOAL #2:						YES. I Decluttered my home office for 30 Minutes	

WEEK #3

GOAL #1:

I will reduce the numbers of hours I work per week by staying at work no later than 7pm or 8pm every night and by leaving work at 4pm at least one day a week to play basketball for a minimum of 1 hour (I will also play basketball for at least one hour on Saturday or Sunday).

GOAL #2:

I will schedule Saturday mornings at 11am as my weekly time to declutter my office space at home.

GOAL #3:

I will schedule Monday mornings at 8am and Thursday mornings at 8am as my weekly times to declutter my office at work.

Anthony Parnell, M.S.W.

	MON	TUE	WED	THU	FRI	SAT	SUN
GOAL #1:		4pm I Left early to play basketball					NO. I did not Play Basketball this weekend.
GOAL #2:						NO. I did not Declutter my home office	
GOAL #3:	YES. I Decluttered my office at work			NO. I did not Declutter my office at work.			

The Self-Help Guide to Stress Management

Reader's Stress Management Goals Chart

WEEK #1

GOAL #1: _____

	MON	TUE	WED	THU	FRI	SAT	SUN
GOAL #1:							

WEEK #2

GOAL #1: _____

GOAL #2: _____

	MON	TUE	WED	THU	FRI	SAT	SUN
GOAL #1:							
GOAL #2:							

Anthony Parnell, M.S.W.

WEEK #3

GOAL #1: _____

GOAL #2: _____

GOAL #3: _____

	MON	TUE	WED	THU	FRI	SAT	SUN
GOAL #1:							
GOAL #2:							
GOAL #3:							

Step Number 4:

Identify Internal and External Resources (that will aid you in accomplishing your goals)

A car may be perfectly built, but it still must receive regular maintenance and check-ups to ensure that it performs at optimal levels. Whether or not an individual has been adequately trained in vehicle maintenance and road performance, once the keys have been handed to the driver, the driver then becomes responsible for the performance and the maintenance of the vehicle.

Some drivers possess unique talents and innate abilities so that they become very good drivers in a relatively short amount of time. Others, though having participated in driver's education and/or

The Self-Help Guide to Stress Management

endured the rigors of driver training, will still lack the confidence to operate the vehicle safely and are in constant fear of an accident.

The analogy of the car is comparable to the Internal and External Resources we possess as we attempt to navigate our way through the maze of life's challenges, abounding with obstacles and adversity. Some individuals are blessed with tremendous health, stamina and adaptive abilities and have acquired a wide range of physical, mental and spiritual outlets. Though possessing valuable internal and external attributes, the resources of other individuals are underutilized or simply undiscovered.

Nevertheless, everyone possesses a particular blend of natural gifts, talents and acquired skills and abilities. Collectively, these can be seen as *strengths* and *current resources*. Without exception, everyone's strengths and current resources can be developed and everyone can identify new resources for further development. This view has direct relevance to Stress Management because these strengths and resources can aid us in the process of maintaining balance and well-being, and more specifically in accomplishing our stress management goals.

"Step Number 3" provided an opportunity for you to begin practicing, visualizing and implementing a routine to ensure that balance and well-being are maintained in your personal and professional lives. "Step Number 4" will assist you in identifying additional tools and resources that will support your efforts to accomplish each of the Prioritized Stress Management Goals listed in "Step #3"; this can also work for future personal and professional goals.

The following was presented at the beginning of this book as the definition of "empowerment."

> *The ability of an individual to utilize the internal and external resources that have been identified to improve one's life situation and to maintain balance and well-being in one's personal and professional lives.*

With the accomplishment of each Prioritized Stress Management Goal, you will discover more about your own empowerment which includes learning to appreciate the resources you possess more fully and deeply. The Stress Management philosophy put forth in this book encourages you to embrace the view that with every endeavor in life, an individual must access his or her internal and external resources for daily survival and to fulfill short-term and long-term goals.

Examples of Internal and External Resources are listed on the following page. After taking a few moments to review, circle any of the Internal and External Resources listed which you feel you possess. Also, feel free to add any other internal or external resources that are not listed.

INTERNAL RESOURCES

Commitment

Discipline

Strong Willed

Faith – Sense of Spirituality

Time Management (Ability to Prioritize)

Positive Attitude/Positive Mindset

Determination

Courage

Persistent

Self-Confidence

Self-Awareness

Being in Tune with One's Body

EXTERNAL RESOURCES

Adequate Transportation

Shelter

Financial Resources to Meet Basic Needs

Social/Emotional Support (Friends, Family)

Extracurricular/Leisure Activities

Gym Membership

Now, having circled the Internal and External Resources which you feel you currently possess:

What Internal and External Resources do you feel you currently possess that can be utilized to accomplish Goal #1 which was previously recorded in Step #3?

Example:

>Goal Statement #1:
>
>I will reduce the numbers of hours I work per week by staying at work no later than 7pm or 8pm every night and by leaving work at 4pm at least one day a week to play basketball for a minimum of 1 hour (I also will play basketball for at least one hour on Saturday or Sunday).
>
>Internal and External Resources:

1. I have a gym membership at 24-Hour Fitness that I can use to play basketball to minimize the potential stress of work overload.
2. I have adequate transportation.
3. I'm highly motivated because I love playing basketball.

Reader:

   Goal Statement #1:

   Internal and External Resources:

1.

2.

3.

What additional Internal and External Resources do you feel you need to develop or obtain to assist you in accomplishing Goal #1?

1.

2.

3.

   Goal Statement #2:

   Internal and External Resources:

What Internal and External Resources do you feel you currently possess that can be utilized to accomplish Goal #2?

1.

2.

3.

What additional Internal and External Resources do you feel you need to develop or obtain to assist you in accomplishing Goal #2?

1.

2.

3.

Goal Statement #3:

Current Internal and External Resources:

What Internal and External Resources do you feel you currently possess that can be utilized to accomplish Goal #3?

1.

2.

3.

What additional Internal and External Resources do you feel you need to develop or obtain to assist you in accomplishing Goal #3?

1.

2.

3.

Step Number 5:

"Putting It All Together" (Maintaining an Effective Stress Management Plan)

You are to be commended for having navigated your way to the end of this book. In reading *The Self-Help Guide to Stress Management* and completing the written exercises, you have strengthened your level of commitment to achieving and maintaining a life of balance and well-being. You have claimed a greater sense of responsibility for your personal growth and for creating the personal and professional lives you envision and greatly desire for yourself.

The greatest challenges now come with sustaining your level of commitment to the "10 Strategies" and finding a minimum of 5 *Minutes a Day* for writing and self-reflection. These are the most essential ingredients for ensuring your success in minimizing stress in your personal and professional lives. In any case, your anxiety should now be minimal. You have been given the necessary tools to be successful in maintaining balance in your personal and professional lives. The "Ten Strategies for Effectively Managing Stress," for example, can be reviewed at any time to identify areas where you may be limiting your ability to minimize stress. Additionally, your "Prioritized Stress Management Goals" can be repeated as many times as needed or revised when presented with new life challenges such as a job transition, relocation or the loss of a loved one.

Additionally, there are a number of resources available in the Appendices. For example, you can utilize the blank charts and writing exercises to create new "Prioritized Stress Management Goals," to record progress with your goals, and to help you maintain greater overall balance. So, do your best to overcome any hesitation or reluctance you may have to refer to any part of this book in the future. You should do so as often as you deem it necessary.

A primary goal of mine in writing *The Self-Help Guide to Stress Management* is to serve as a catalyst for you to utilize writing and self-reflection as a tool for maintaining balance and well-being in your personal and professional lives. Many workshop participants, social work professionals and their clients have successfully utilized and implemented the philosophy and techniques of *The Self-Help Guide to Stress Management*. It is my hope that by reading this book you have increased your level of self-awareness and have already begun to experience decreased levels of stress as you move toward living the life you desire and deserve!

Anthony Parnell, M.S.W.

"Life's Inner Ocean"

Life's Ocean
flowwwsss
through the Spirit of man.

the depth of my soul
reaches the depth of the ocean.

this is where my inner peace
is found....
in my soul.

knowing that I am in harmony
with The Divine Universe,
that I have connected with that deeper source
of spirituality, peace and balance.

to see beyond The Moment.

to see beyond what physically lies
within my eyesight
to see what is unfolding
spiritually....

that peace is being found
not in things.....
but in Life's Infinite Ocean of Spirit
that flowwwssss through me.

Anthony Parnell

APPENDIX A

SELF-EXPLORATORY QUESTIONS

Have there been any significant changes in your behavior?

If yes, what significant changes have occurred in your behavior?

How long ago do you recall these significant changes occurring in your behavior?

Are your daily thoughts focused on the past or the future rather than on the current moment?

Has there been a significant decline in the number of completed tasks at home or work?

If yes, when did the decline in the number of completed tasks begin to occur?

Have you experienced a significant decrease in your level of energy?

If yes, when did you begin to feel a significant decrease in your level of energy?

Is there a consistent or frequent feeling of panic or frustration that you will never be able to catch up – that there are always tasks left unfinished that really need to be completed?

Is there added clutter in your home and/or work environment?

Do friends, relatives or peers constantly tell you that you are stressed?

Are you embarrassed to ask for help to get reorganized?

APPENDIX B

Stress Management Report Card

The Self-Help Guide to Stress Management

STRESS MANAGEMENT REPORT CARD (Self-Graded)

ELEMENTS	GRADE
Strategy Number 1: Accept that Stress Management is a Lifestyle that Requires an Individual to be Proactive rather than Reactive	
Strategy Number 2: Be Consistent in Setting Aside an Adequate Amount of Time to be Alone and in Silence (for Self-Reflection)	
Strategy Number 3: Be Honest with Yourself on a Daily Basis and in All Situations	
Strategy Number 4: Accept that Balance Can Be Achieved Only When There is an Equal Commitment to Your Mind, Body and Spirit	
Strategy Number 5: Exercise Discipline in Working towards Large Goals By First Disciplining Yourself in Accomplishing Small Goals	
Strategy Number 6: Maintain Balance in Your Personal and professional lives by Identifying and Utilizing Tangible and Intangible Resources (Physical, Social, Psychological, Material)	
Strategy Number 7: Minimize Physical Clutter in Your Home and Workplace	
Strategy Number 8: Be Consistent in Surrounding Yourself and Interacting with Positive People	
Strategy Number 9: Financially Prepare for Economic Downturns, Job Layoffs, and/or Retirement	
Strategy Number 10: Develop an Emergency Preparedness Plan in the Event of a Natural Disaster and/or Other Unexpected Environmental, National or Global Crisis	

APPENDIX C

5 Minutes a Day of Writing & Self-Reflection"

	SUN.	MON.	TUE.	WED.	THU.	FRI.	SAT.
Week #1							
Week #2							
Week #3							
Week #4							
Week #5							
Week #6							

APPENDIX D

SAMPLE MAINTENANCE PLAN FOR DECLUTTERING PHYSICAL ENVIRONMENT

15-30 MINUTES A DAY	SUN	MON	TUE	WED	THU	FRI	SAT
Day #1 Monday							
Day #2 Thursday							

SAMPLE MAINTENANCE PLAN FOR DECLUTTERING PHYSICAL ENVIRONMENT

Designated Time: 8am

Designated days per week (2): Monday and Thursday

SAMPLE

Week #1

15-30 MINUTES A DAY	SUN	MON	TUE	WED	THU	FRI	SAT
Day #1 Monday		Yes 15 Min.					
Day #2 Thursday					No		

Week #2

15-30 MINUTES A DAY	SUN	MON	TUE	WED	THU	FRI	SAT
Day #1 Monday		No					
Day #2 Thursday					Yes		

Week #3

15-30 MINUTES A DAY	SUN	MON	TUE	WED	THU	FRI	SAT
Day #1 Monday		Yes 20 Min.					
Day #2 Thursday					Yes 30 Min.		

The Self-Help Guide to Stress Management

READER'S MAINTENANCE PLAN FOR DECLUTTERING PHYSICAL ENVIRONMENT

Designated Time _____ am/pm

Designated days per week (2): _____

READER's PLAN

Week #1

15-30 MINUTES A DAY	SUN	MON	TUE	WED	THU	FRI	SAT
Day #1 _____							
Day #2 _____							

Anthony Parnell, M.S.W.

Week #2

15-30 MINUTES A DAY	SUN	MON	TUE	WED	THU	FRI	SAT
Day #1 _____							
Day #2 _____							

Week #3

15-30 MINUTES A DAY	SUN	MON	TUE	WED	THU	FRI	SAT
Day #1 _____							
Day #2 _____							

Feelings of helplessness and being overwhelmed can easily be triggered when we see lots of clutter in our physical environment. But the feeling of being overwhelmed can suddenly be transformed to a feeling of empowerment and lightheartedness when the clutter is removed. Unfortunately, once you begin to experience emotional and physical fatigue, your energy is zapped by the constant bombardments that interfere with keeping pace with the increasing demands placed on your time and energy. It then can become even more challenging to find the time and the energy to remove the piles of clutter that have accumulated in the spaces where you live and work. For this reason, it is very important to maintain a commitment to removing the physical clutter on a consistent or daily basis.

The same approach to decluttering your thoughts and emotions, as outlined in "Step Number 1," needs to be utilized when contemplating how and where to begin in "Decluttering Your Physical Environment;" and, just as piles of clutter accumulate over time, it must be understood that a significant amount of time will be required for the task of decluttering. Therefore, it is strongly recommended that you begin by committing to Decluttering your Physical Environment for Fifteen to Thirty Minutes a Day for Five Consecutive Days.

Initially, this modest investment of time and effort will allow you to feel an immediate sense of personal accomplishment. Secondly, as shared earlier in Strategy #5 ("Exercise Discipline in Working towards Large Goals By First Disciplining Yourself in Accomplishing

Small Goals"), it will ensure that you set realistic expectations in an effort to restore a sense of open space and positive energy in your physical environment.

If you have family, friends or a professional organizer to assist you in your decluttering, it would be perfectly okay to begin with more than Fifteen to Thirty Minutes A Day. Otherwise, do not overexert yourself in an attempt to accomplish too much too soon. Rather, be content with taking small steps to achieve some sense of forward progress. And, as you begin to gain confidence and to feel revitalized, slowly increase the amount of time spent each day decluttering your physical environment.

It's easy to understand why someone might argue that the most important area to begin decluttering is the area that has the greatest amount of clutter or that causes the greatest amount of stress in their life. I, however, recommend selecting a room or area that is the least stressful or the easiest to declutter so as to quickly feel a sense of accomplishment. This cannot do anything but help instill more confidence for subsequent efforts! Then, once you have been successful in removing clutter from one room or area, continue to apply the same strategy to other rooms or areas, one at a time. Equally important, once the home or work environment has been completely decluttered, it is vital that you commit to setting a time, a minimum of 15-30 minutes, at least one or two days a week, so that you can maintain your newly acquired sense of openness and "flow."

The Self-Help Guide to Stress Management

Incorporating a maintenance or prevention plan will ensure that you do not become overwhelmed again by piles of clutter. This requires discipline and an acceptance that maintaining balance is a continuous process.

The philosophy of committing to Fifteen to Thirty Minutes A Day has even greater relevance because of the reciprocal relationship that exists between decluttering one's thoughts and emotions and decluttering one's physical environment. They directly influence one another. Even though there are some individuals who possess the ability to function at high levels with a cluttered physical environment or cluttered thoughts and emotions, this is not true for most of us. Over time, most individuals are unable to maximize their emotional and spiritual growth and sense of balance and well-being without strengthening their mental resources and securing their immediate surroundings.

Gradual steps are required to achieve balance and well-being in your personal and professional lives. Consequently, if you are feeling overwhelmed by the clutter that has accumulated around you, be honest in accepting how you are feeling. If needed, ask for help from family, friends or hire a professional organizer (see "Additional Resources"). Also, books on decluttering and personal organizing can be very helpful.

Some professional organizers are opposed to storing personal belongings and other items until a later date when there would be adequate time to sort through the items. Personally, I have, on occasion, used this strategy with some success. In doing so, I simply placed piles of cluttered items and belongings that currently were not being utilized into boxes and filing cabinets. Admittedly, this is a temporary solution. However, this strategy has at times provided me with a sense of relief and an increased ability to concentrate more effectively on the current priorities in my personal and professional lives. At the same time, it created a greater sense of open space in my physical environment, which made me feel more relaxed and comfortable. Fortunately, I did exercise the discipline to adhere to the date and time I set to return to the piles of clutter in storage and resume the process of decluttering.

Charts have been provided for you to record your progress in implementing 1) an initial plan, and 2) a maintenance plan, for decluttering your physical environment at home or work.

Here are two important questions that you should first ask before beginning the actual work of decluttering your physical environment.

1. **What time of day is best for you to focus your energy on decluttering your home environment?**

2. **What room or area of your home or office will you initially focus and concentrate your time and energy on in order to declutter your physical environment?**

APPENDIX E

Self-Care Monitoring Chart

	5 MINUTES ALONE	ADEQUATE AMOUNT OF SLEEP	HEALTHY DIET	EXTRACURRICULAR ACTIVITIES
SUNDAY				
MONDAY				
TUESDAY				
WEDNESDAY				
THURSDAY				
FRIDAY				
SATURDAY				
SUNDAY				
MONDAY				
TUESDAY				
WEDNESDAY				
THURSDAY				
FRIDAY				
SATURDAY				

APPENDIX F

Affirmations for Minimizing Stress

I am calm and relaxed.
Only positive energy and positive people are attracted into my life.

~

Because I accept that Stress is a part of life,
I am committing to setting aside
a minimum of "5 Minutes a Day" of writing and self-reflection
to help me maintain the highest level of self-awareness.

~

I am one and in harmony
with peace, comfort and well-being.

~

I am surrounded by people, places and things that energize me.

~

My thoughts are positive.
My actions are positive.
As a result,
the outcomes I manifest in my life
are positive.

APPENDIX G

*Exercise for Surrounding Yourself
with Positive People*

The accumulation of mental, emotional and physical clutter robs an individual of his or her energy and the ability to maintain balance and well-being. Cluttered relationships can also serve as an additional roadblock to personal growth, balance, and well-being. Yet, few individuals are willing to be completely honest or to carefully examine the negative impact of relationships that take more energy than they give to the individual.

Learning to set healthy boundaries with family and friends (which includes learning how and when to say "No!") can be a very challenging and painful process. Many individuals compete with intense feelings of guilt when faced with constant requests for time, energy and even money. This is often due to the fact that many live by the belief that they must be willing to sacrifice anything and everything for loved ones no matter the circumstances or the consequences. Yet, without realizing it, an individual may be blinded by his or her personal beliefs, and also fail to realize that family and friends do not share the same values or discipline. Consequently, although there is reciprocating love and respect, these people are not willing to make the same sacrifices and compromises.

Tremendous effort is required in learning to make distinctions between relationships that drain your energy and those that motivate and inspire you. Self-awareness and honesty with yourself are necessary ingredients. You must recognize and accept that (similar to changing bad habits), individuals, over time, will develop a set of expectations based on past experiences. By expanding your self-awareness and increasing your sense of personal responsibility and discipline, you will be better able to determine the boundaries that are necessary for healthy relationships and know how to consistently maintain those boundaries once they have been established.

The conscious commitment of an individual to constantly surround his or herself with positive people, places and things is a defining moment in a life. It is a spiritual milestone, signifying an attempt to accept complete responsibility for shaping the direction of their life, both personally and professionally. This defining moment, then, becomes a commitment that will not succumb to social or environmental pressures (e.g., the pressure to befriend or associate oneself with individuals who are not like-minded or like-spirited). Ultimately, it represents a transitional period in life in which an individual gains a renewed sense of clarity about his or her beliefs and values by discovering and fully embracing the courage and strength required to follow his or her own unique path.

Using the worksheet below, take a few moments to create a list of the positive people who energize and inspire you. Then, simply make a conscious effort to increase the amount of time you spend surrounded by these positive people.

MY PERSONAL LIST OF POSITIVE PEOPLE WHO ENERGIZE AND INSPIRE ME

APPENDIX H

7 Key Elements to Organizational Change

7 KEY ELEMENTS TO ORGANIZATIONAL CHANGE National Institute for Occupational and Safety and Health (1999) *Stress at work* (page 15).	GRADE
1. Ensure that the workload is in line with Workers' capabilities and resources.	
2. Design jobs to provide meaning, stimulation, and opportunities for workers to use their skills.	
3. Clearly define workers' roles and responsibilities.	
4. Give workers opportunities to participate in decisions and actions affecting their jobs.	
5. Improve communication – reduce uncertainty about career development and future employment prospects.	
6. Provide opportunities for social interaction among workers.	
7. Establish work schedules that are compatible with demands and responsibilities outside the job.	

APPENDIX I

Eight Variables Related to Job Satisfaction and Functioning Effectively in the Workplace

EIGHT VARIABLES RELATED TO JOB SATISFACTION AND FUNCTIONING EFFECTIVELY IN THE WORKPLACE Karl Albrecht, (2008). *Stress and the manager: Making it work for you* (p. 139)	GRADE
1. Workload	
2. Physical Variables	
3. Job Status	
4. Accountability	
5. Task Variety	
6. Human Contact	
7. Physical Challenge	
8. Mental Challenge	

Notes

Anthony Parnell, M.S.W.

Notes

Additional Resources

Websites:

www.apa.org (American Psychological Association) Information on stress and other health related questions.

> https://www.apa.org/topics/stress/index.html APA. Stress Facts and Tips; How to Cope with and Identify Stress; The Science of Stress. Practitioner well-being.

> https://www.apa.org/helpcenter/stress. APA. "Stress on the Body" (Visual Simulation)

> www.StressinAmerica.org

www.cdc.gov/niosh The National Institute for Occupational Safety and Health (NIOSH) offers more detailed information about job stress. Additionally, NIOSH, as part of the Centers for Disease Control and Prevention (CDC) is the Federal agency responsible for conducting research and making recommendations for the prevention of work-related illness and injury. As part of its mandate, NIOSH works with industry, labor and academia to better understand the stress of modern work, the effects of stress on safety and health, and ways to reduce stress in the workplace. NIOSH can also be contacted by phone at 1-800-232-4636 or by email at https://www.cdc.gov/niosh/contact/default.html.

The Self-Help Guide to Stress Management

https://www.helpguide.org/home-pages/stress-management.htm
A detailed outline of stress warning signs and symptoms (behavioral, cognitive, emotional, and physical) and other health related questions.

https://www.helpguide.org/?s=stress+warning+signs

- *Stress Symptoms, Signs, and Causes*
- *Stress Management*
- *Stress in the Workplace*
- *Stress and Your Health*
- *Quick Stress Relief*
- *Traumatic Stress*
- *Burnout Prevention and Treatment*
- *Prevention*

www.medicinenet.com A detailed outline of stress warning signs and symptoms and other health related questions.

www.napo.net (National Association of Professional Organizers) Professional assistance in decluttering and organizing your home and work environment.

Anthony Parnell, M.S.W.

Locating a Psychologist or Mental Health Professional in Your Area:

For a list of consultants in your area who specialize in job stress, contact the American Psychological Association (APA) 1-800-374-2721 (https://locator.apa.org/).

Licensed Mental Health Therapists; Contact the Board of Behavioral Science Examiners for your state or look in the yellow pages under Mental Health Information, Psychologists and Psychotherapists.

The National Suicide Prevention Lifeline:

A 24-hour, toll-free suicide prevention service available to anyone in suicidal crisis. If you need help, please dial **1-800-273-8255**. With over 150 crisis centers across the country, you will be routed to the closest possible crisis center in your area. www.suicidepreventionlifeline.org

www.ncdc.noaa.gov (National Centers for Environmental Information)

www.ourworldindata.org (Our World in Data (ourworldindata.org)

References and Further Reading

Albrecht, K. (2008). *Stress and the manager: Making it work for you.* Simon & Schuster.

American Psychological Association. (2017). *Stress in America: Coping with change.* Stress in America™ Survey.

American Psychological Association. (2019). *Stress in America: Stress and current events.* Stress in America™ Survey.

Gawain, S. (2002) *Creative visualization: Use the power of your imagination to create what you want in your life.* New World Library.

Goldway, E. M. (1997). *Inner balance: The power of holistic healing: Insights of Hans Selye, Elisabeth Kubler-Ross, Marcus Bach, and others.* Prentice-Hall.

Murphy, J. (2000). *The power of your subconscious mind.* Bantam Books.

National Centers for Environmental Information. www.ncdc.noaa.gov

National Institute for Occupational and Safety and Health. (1999). *Stress at work* (NIOSH Publication No. 99-101). U. S. Government Printing Office.

National Institute for Occupational and Safety and Health. (2002). *Working with stress* (NIOSH Publication No. 2003-114d. U. S.) Government Printing Office.

Orman, S. (2002). *The courage to be rich*. Riverhead Books.

Orman, S. (2004). *The laws of money: 5 timeless secrets to get out and stay out of financial trouble.* Free Press.

Our World in Data. www.ourworldindata.org

Parnell, A. (2005). Healing through writing: A journaling guide to emotional and spiritual growth. iUniverse.

Selye, H. (1956). *The stress of life.* McGraw-Hill.

Selye, H. (1978). *The stress of life* (2nd ed.) McGraw-Hill.

Selye, H. (1974). *Stress without distress.* Lippincottt.

Wood, S. E., Wood, E. G., & Boyd, D. (2004) *Mastering the world of psychology.* Pearson.

About the Author

Anthony Parnell, M.S.W. is a Stress Management Trainer, Entrepreneur Coach and Author of several books. He resides in Las Vegas, Nevada.

www.AnthonyParnell.com

www.EntrepreneursApex.com